# Love Songs

# Love Songs
## Sara Teasdale

MINT EDITIONS

*Love Songs* was first published in 1917.

This edition published by Mint Editions 2021.

ISBN 9781513295923 | E-ISBN 9781513297422

Published by Mint Editions®

 MINT
EDITIONS

minteditionbooks.com

Publishing Director: Jennifer Newens
Design & Production: Rachel Lopez Metzger
Project Manager: Micaela Clark
Typesetting: Westchester Publishing Services

# Contents

IV

A November Night

I

# BARTER

Life has loveliness to sell,
    All beautiful and splendid things,
Blue waves whitened on a cliff,
    Soaring fire that sways and sings,
And children's faces looking up
Holding wonder like a cup.

Life has loveliness to sell,
    Music like a curve of gold,
Scent of pine trees in the rain,
    Eyes that love you, arms that hold,
And for your spirit's still delight,
Holy thoughts that star the night.

Spend all you have for loveliness,
    Buy it and never count the cost;
For one white singing hour of peace
    Count many a year of strife well lost,
And for a breath of ecstasy
Give all you have been, or could be.

# Twilight

Dreamily over the roofs
    The cold spring rain is falling;
Out in the lonely tree
    A bird is calling, calling.

Slowly over the earth
    The wings of night are falling;
My heart like the bird in the tree
    Is calling, calling, calling.

SARA TEASDALE

# Night Song at Amalfi

I asked the heaven of stars
    What I should give my love—
It answered me with silence,
    Silence above.

I asked the darkened sea
    Down where the fishers go—
It answered me with silence,
    Silence below.

Oh, I could give him weeping,
    Or I could give him song—
But how can I give silence,
    My whole life long?

# THE LOOK

Strephon kissed me in the spring,
　　Robin in the fall,
But Colin only looked at me
　　And never kissed at all.

Strephon's kiss was lost in jest,
　　Robin's lost in play,
But the kiss in Colin's eyes
　　Haunts me night and day.

# A Winter Night

My window-pane is starred with frost,
    The world is bitter cold tonight,
The moon is cruel, and the wind
    Is like a two-edged sword to smite.

God pity all the homeless ones,
    The beggars pacing to and fro,
God pity all the poor tonight
    Who walk the lamp-lit streets of snow.

My room is like a bit of June,
    Warm and close-curtained fold on fold,
But somewhere, like a homeless child,
    My heart is crying in the cold.

# A Cry

Oh, there are eyes that he can see,
    And hands to make his hands rejoice,
But to my lover I must be
    Only a voice.

Oh, there are breasts to bear his head,
    And lips whereon his lips can lie,
But I must be till I am dead
    Only a cry.

# Gifts

I gave my first love laughter,
   I gave my second tears,
I gave my third love silence
   Through all the years.

My first love gave me singing,
   My second eyes to see,
But oh, it was my third love
   Who gave my soul to me.

# But Not to Me

The April night is still and sweet
    With flowers on every tree;
Peace comes to them on quiet feet,
      But not to me.

My peace is hidden in his breast
    Where I shall never be;
Love comes tonight to all the rest,
      But not to me.

SARA TEASDALE

# Song at Capri

When beauty grows too great to bear
    How shall I ease me of its ache,
For beauty more than bitterness
    Makes the heart break.

Now while I watch the dreaming sea
    With isles like flowers against her breast,
Only one voice in all the world
    Could give me rest.

# CHILD, CHILD

Child, child, love while you can
The voice and the eyes and the soul of a man;
Never fear though it break your heart—
Out of the wound new joy will start;
Only love proudly and gladly and well,
Though love be heaven or love be hell.

Child, child, love while you may,
For life is short as a happy day;
Never fear the thing you feel—
Only by love is life made real;
Love, for the deadly sins are seven,
Only through love will you enter heaven.

# LOVE ME

Brown-thrush singing all day long
    In the leaves above me,
Take my love this April song,
    "Love me, love me, love me!"

When he harkens what you say,
    Bid him, lest he miss me,
Leave his work or leave his play,
    And kiss me, kiss me, kiss me!

# PIERROT

Pierrot stands in the garden
    Beneath a waning moon,
And on his lute he fashions
    A fragile silver tune.

Pierrot plays in the garden,
    He thinks he plays for me,
But I am quite forgotten
    Under the cherry tree.

Pierrot plays in the garden,
    And all the roses know
That Pierrot loves his music,—
    But I love Pierrot.

# WILD ASTERS

In the spring I asked the daisies
    If his words were true,
And the clever, clear-eyed daisies
    Always knew.

Now the fields are brown and barren,
    Bitter autumn blows,
And of all the stupid asters
    Not one knows.

# The Song for Colin

I sang a song at dusking time
    Beneath the evening star,
And Terence left his latest rhyme
    To answer from afar.

Pierrot laid down his lute to weep,
    And sighed, "She sings for me."
But Colin slept a careless sleep
    Beneath an apple tree.

# FOUR WINDS

"Four winds blowing through the sky,
You have seen poor maidens die,
Tell me then what I shall do
That my lover may be true."
Said the wind from out the south,
"Lay no kiss upon his mouth,"
And the wind from out the west,
"Wound the heart within his breast,"
And the wind from out the east,
"Send him empty from the feast,"
And the wind from out the north,
"In the tempest thrust him forth;
When thou art more cruel than he,
Then will Love be kind to thee."

# Debt

What do I owe to you
    Who loved me deep and long?
You never gave my spirit wings
    Or gave my heart a song.

But oh, to him I loved,
    Who loved me not at all,
I owe the open gate
    That led through heaven's wall.

SARA TEASDALE

# FAULTS

They came to tell your faults to me,
They named them over one by one;
I laughed aloud when they were done,
I knew them all so well before,—
Oh, they were blind, too blind to see
Your faults had made me love you more.

# BURIED LOVE

I have come to bury Love
    Beneath a tree,
In the forest tall and black
    Where none can see.

I shall put no flowers at his head,
    Nor stone at his feet,
For the mouth I loved so much
    Was bittersweet.

I shall go no more to his grave,
    For the woods are cold.
I shall gather as much of joy
    As my hands can hold.

I shall stay all day in the sun
    Where the wide winds blow,—
But oh, I shall cry at night
    When none will know.

# THE FOUNTAIN

All through the deep blue night
    The fountain sang alone;
It sang to the drowsy heart
    Of the satyr carved in stone.

The fountain sang and sang,
    But the satyr never stirred—
Only the great white moon
    In the empty heaven heard.

The fountain sang and sang
    While on the marble rim
The milk-white peacocks slept,
    And their dreams were strange and dim.

Bright dew was on the grass,
    And on the ilex, dew,
The dreamy milk-white birds
    Were all a-glisten, too.

The fountain sang and sang
    The things one cannot tell;
The dreaming peacocks stirred
    And the gleaming dew-drops fell.

# I SHALL NOT CARE

When I am dead and over me bright April
    Shakes out her rain-drenched hair,
Though you should lean above me broken-hearted,
    I shall not care.

I shall have peace, as leafy trees are peaceful
    When rain bends down the bough,
And I shall be more silent and cold-hearted
    Than you are now.

# AFTER PARTING

Oh, I have sown my love so wide
    That he will find it everywhere;
It will awake him in the night,
    It will enfold him in the air.

I set my shadow in his sight
    And I have winged it with desire,
That it may be a cloud by day,
    And in the night a shaft of fire.

# A Prayer

Until I lose my soul and lie
    Blind to the beauty of the earth,
Deaf though shouting wind goes by,
    Dumb in a storm of mirth;

Until my heart is quenched at length
    And I have left the land of men,
Oh, let me love with all my strength
    Careless if I am loved again.

SARA TEASDALE

# SPRING NIGHT

The park is filled with night and fog,
    The veils are drawn about the world,
The drowsy lights along the paths
    Are dim and pearled.

Gold and gleaming the empty streets,
    Gold and gleaming the misty lake,
The mirrored lights like sunken swords,
    Glimmer and shake.

Oh, is it not enough to be
Here with this beauty over me?
My throat should ache with praise, and I
Should kneel in joy beneath the sky.
O, beauty, are you not enough?
Why am I crying after love,
With youth, a singing voice, and eyes
To take earth's wonder with surprise?

Why have I put off my pride,
Why am I unsatisfied,—
I, for whom the pensive night
Binds her cloudy hair with light,—
I, for whom all beauty burns
Like incense in a million urns?
O beauty, are you not enough?
Why am I crying after love?

# MAY WIND

I said, "I have shut my heart
　　As one shuts an open door,
That Love may starve therein
　　And trouble me no more."

But over the roofs there came
　　The wet new wind of May,
And a tune blew up from the curb
　　Where the street-pianos play.

My room was white with the sun
　　And Love cried out in me,
"I am strong, I will break your heart
　　Unless you set me free."

# Tides

Love in my heart was a fresh tide flowing
    Where the starlike sea gulls soar;
The sun was keen and the foam was blowing
    High on the rocky shore.

But now in the dusk the tide is turning,
    Lower the sea gulls soar,
And the waves that rose in resistless yearning
    Are broken forevermore.

# After Love

There is no magic any more,
    We meet as other people do,
You work no miracle for me
    Nor I for you.

You were the wind and I the sea—
    There is no splendor any more,
I have grown listless as the pool
    Beside the shore.

But though the pool is safe from storm
    And from the tide has found surcease,
It grows more bitter than the sea,
    For all its peace.

SARA TEASDALE

# New Love and Old

In my heart the old love
    Struggled with the new;
It was ghostly waking
    All night through.

Dear things, kind things,
    That my old love said,
Ranged themselves reproachfully
    Round my bed.

But I could not heed them,
    For I seemed to see
The eyes of my new love
    Fixed on me.

Old love, old love,
    How can I be true?
Shall I be faithless to myself
    Or to you?

# THE KISS

I hoped that he would love me,
    And he has kissed my mouth,
But I am like a stricken bird
    That cannot reach the south.

For though I know he loves me,
    Tonight my heart is sad;
His kiss was not so wonderful
    As all the dreams I had.

# SWANS

Night is over the park, and a few brave stars
    Look on the lights that link it with chains of gold,
The lake bears up their reflection in broken bars
    That seem too heavy for tremulous water to hold.

We watch the swans that sleep in a shadowy place,
    And now and again one wakes and uplifts its head;
How still you are—your gaze is on my face—
    We watch the swans and never a word is said.

# The River

I came from the sunny valleys
    And sought for the open sea,
For I thought in its gray expanses
    My peace would come to me.

I came at last to the ocean
    And found it wild and black,
And I cried to the windless valleys,
    "Be kind and take me back!"

But the thirsty tide ran inland,
    And the salt waves drank of me,
And I who was fresh as the rainfall
    Am bitter as the sea.

# November

The world is tired, the year is old,
　　The fading leaves are glad to die,
The wind goes shivering with cold
　　Where the brown reeds are dry.

Our love is dying like the grass,
　　And we who kissed grow coldly kind,
Half glad to see our old love pass
　　Like leaves along the wind.

# Spring Rain

I thought I had forgotten,
　　But it all came back again
Tonight with the first spring thunder
　　In a rush of rain.

I remembered a darkened doorway
　　Where we stood while the storm swept by,
Thunder gripping the earth
　　And lightning scrawled on the sky.

The passing motor busses swayed,
　　For the street was a river of rain,
Lashed into little golden waves
　　In the lamp light's stain.

With the wild spring rain and thunder
　　My heart was wild and gay;
Your eyes said more to me that night
　　Than your lips would ever say. . .

I thought I had forgotten,
　　But it all came back again
Tonight with the first spring thunder
　　In a rush of rain.

# THE GHOST

I went back to the clanging city,
    I went back where my old loves stayed,
But my heart was full of my new love's glory,
    My eyes were laughing and unafraid.

I met one who had loved me madly
    And told his love for all to hear—
But we talked of a thousand things together,
    The past was buried too deep to fear.

I met the other, whose love was given
    With never a kiss and scarcely a word—
Oh, it was then the terror took me
    Of words unuttered that breathed and stirred.

Oh, love that lives its life with laughter
    Or love that lives its life with tears
Can die—but love that is never spoken
    Goes like a ghost through the winding years. . .

I went back to the clanging city,
    I went back where my old loves stayed,
My heart was full of my new love's glory,—
    But my eyes were suddenly afraid.

# Summer Night, Riverside

In the wild, soft summer darkness
How many and many a night we two together
Sat in the park and watched the Hudson
Wearing her lights like golden spangles
Glinting on black satin.
The rail along the curving pathway
Was low in a happy place to let us cross,
And down the hill a tree that dripped with bloom
Sheltered us,
While your kisses and the flowers,
Falling, falling,
Tangled my hair. . .


The frail white stars moved slowly over the sky.


And now, far off
In the fragrant darkness
The tree is tremulous again with bloom,
For June comes back.

Tonight what girl
Dreamily before her mirror shakes from her hair
This year's blossoms, clinging in its coils?

# Jewels

If I should see your eyes again,
    I know how far their look would go—
Back to a morning in the park
    With sapphire shadows on the snow.

Or back to oak trees in the spring
    When you unloosed my hair and kissed
The head that lay against your knees
    In the leaf shadow's amethyst.

And still another shining place
    We would remember—how the dun
Wild mountain held us on its crest
    One diamond morning white with sun.

But I will turn my eyes from you
    As women turn to put away
The jewels they have worn at night
    And cannot wear in sober day.

## II

## INTERLUDE: SONGS OUT OF SORROW

# I

## SPIRIT'S HOUSE

From naked stones of agony
I will build a house for me;
As a mason all alone
I will raise it, stone by stone,
And every stone where I have bled
Will show a sign of dusky red.
I have not gone the way in vain,
For I have good of all my pain;
My spirit's quiet house will be
Built of naked stones I trod
On roads where I lost sight of God.

## MASTERY

I would not have a god come in
To shield me suddenly from sin,
And set my house of life to rights;
Nor angels with bright burning wings
Ordering my earthly thoughts and things;
Rather my own frail guttering lights
Wind blown and nearly beaten out;
Rather the terror of the nights
And long, sick groping after doubt;
Rather be lost than let my soul
Slip vaguely from my own control—
Of my own spirit let me be
In sole though feeble mastery.

# III

## Lessons

Unless I learn to ask no help
    From any other soul but mine,
To seek no strength in waving reeds
    Nor shade beneath a straggling pine;
Unless I learn to look at Grief
    Unshrinking from her tear-blind eyes,
And take from Pleasure fearlessly
    Whatever gifts will make me wise—
Unless I learn these things on earth,
Why was I ever given birth?

# IV

## Wisdom

When I have ceased to break my wings
Against the faultiness of things,
And learned that compromises wait
Behind each hardly opened gate,
When I can look Life in the eyes,
Grown calm and very coldly wise,
Life will have given me the Truth,
And taken in exchange—my youth.

# V

## In a Burying Ground

This is the spot where I will lie
    When life has had enough of me,
These are the grasses that will blow
    Above me like a living sea.

These gay old lilies will not shrink
    To draw their life from death of mine,
And I will give my body's fire
    To make blue flowers on this vine.

"O Soul," I said, "have you no tears?
    Was not the body dear to you?"
I heard my soul say carelessly,
    "The myrtle flowers will grow more blue."

## VI

## Wood Song

I heard a wood thrush in the dusk
    Twirl three notes and make a star—
My heart that walked with bitterness
    Came back from very far.

Three shining notes were all he had,
    And yet they made a starry call—
I caught life back against my breast
    And kissed it, scars and all.

# VII

## Refuge

From my spirit's gray defeat,
From my pulse's flagging beat,
From my hopes that turned to sand
Sifting through my close-clenched hand,
From my own fault's slavery,
If I can sing, I still am free.

For with my singing I can make
A refuge for my spirit's sake,
A house of shining words, to be
My fragile immortality.

III

# The Flight

Look back with longing eyes and know that I will follow,
Lift me up in your love as a light wind lifts a swallow,
Let our flight be far in sun or blowing rain—
*But what if I heard my first love calling me again?*

Hold me on your heart as the brave sea holds the foam,
Take me far away to the hills that hide your home;
Peace shall thatch the roof and love shall latch the door—
*But what if I heard my first love calling me once more?*

# DEW

As dew leaves the cobweb lightly
 Threaded with stars,
Scattering jewels on the fence
 And the pasture bars;
As dawn leaves the dry grass bright
 And the tangled weeds
Bearing a rainbow gem
 On each of their seeds;
So has your love, my lover,
 Fresh as the dawn,
Made me a shining road
 To travel on,
Set every common sight
 Of tree or stone
Delicately alight
 For me alone.

# TONIGHT

The moon is a curving flower of gold,
    The sky is still and blue;
The moon was made for the sky to hold,
    And I for you.

The moon is a flower without a stem,
    The sky is luminous;
Eternity was made for them,
    Tonight for us.

# Ebb Tide

When the long day goes by
    And I do not see your face,
The old wild, restless sorrow
    Steals from its hiding place.

My day is barren and broken,
    Bereft of light and song,
A sea beach bleak and windy
    That moans the whole day long.

To the empty beach at ebb tide,
    Bare with its rocks and scars,
Come back like the sea with singing,
    And light of a million stars.

SARA TEASDALE

# I Would Live in Your Love

I would live in your love as the sea-grasses live in the sea,
Borne up by each wave as it passes, drawn down by each wave that
    recedes;
I would empty my soul of the dreams that have gathered in me,
I would beat with your heart as it beats, I would follow your soul as it
    leads.

# BECAUSE

Oh, because you never tried
To bow my will or break my pride,
And nothing of the cave-man made
You want to keep me half afraid,
Nor ever with a conquering air
You thought to draw me unaware—
Take me, for I love you more
Than I ever loved before.

And since the body's maidenhood
Alone were neither rare nor good
Unless with it I gave to you
A spirit still untrammeled, too,
Take my dreams and take my mind
That were masterless as wind;
And "Master!" I shall say to you
Since you never asked me to.

# The Tree of Song

I sang my songs for the rest,
    For you I am still;
The tree of my song is bare
    On its shining hill.

For you came like a lordly wind,
    And the leaves were whirled
Far as forgotten things
    Past the rim of the world.

The tree of my song stands bare
    Against the blue—
I gave my songs to the rest,
    Myself to you.

# THE GIVER

You bound strong sandals on my feet,
    You gave me bread and wine,
And sent me under sun and stars,
    For all the world was mine.

Oh, take the sandals off my feet,
    You know not what you do;
For all my world is in your arms,
    My sun and stars are you.

# APRIL SONG

Willow, in your April gown
    Delicate and gleaming,
Do you mind in years gone by
    All my dreaming?

Spring was like a call to me
    That I could not answer,
I was chained to loneliness,
    I, the dancer.

Willow, twinkling in the sun,
    Still your leaves and hear me,
I can answer spring at last,
    Love is near me!

# THE WANDERER

I saw the sunset-colored sands,
    The Nile like flowing fire between,
    Where Rameses stares forth serene,
And Ammon's heavy temple stands.

I saw the rocks where long ago,
    Above the sea that cries and breaks,
    Swift Perseus with Medusa's snakes
Set free the maiden white like snow.

And many skies have covered me,
    And many winds have blown me forth,
    And I have loved the green, bright north,
And I have loved the cold, sweet sea.

But what to me are north and south,
    And what the lure of many lands,
    Since you have leaned to catch my hands
And lay a kiss upon my mouth.

# THE YEARS

Tonight I close my eyes and see
A strange procession passing me—
The years before I saw your face
Go by me with a wistful grace;
They pass, the sensitive, shy years,
As one who strives to dance, half blind with tears.

The years went by and never knew
That each one brought me nearer you;
Their path was narrow and apart
And yet it led me to your heart—
Oh, sensitive, shy years, oh, lonely years,
That strove to sing with voices drowned in tears.

# Enough

It is enough for me by day
    To walk the same bright earth with him;
Enough that over us by night
    The same great roof of stars is dim.

I do not hope to bind the wind
    Or set a fetter on the sea—
It is enough to feel his love
    Blow by like music over me.

# Come

Come, when the pale moon like a petal
    Floats in the pearly dusk of spring,
Come with arms outstretched to take me,
    Come with lips pursed up to cling.

Come, for life is a frail moth flying,
    Caught in the web of the years that pass,
And soon we two, so warm and eager,
    Will be as the gray stones in the grass.

# JOY

I am wild, I will sing to the trees,
    I will sing to the stars in the sky,
I love, I am loved, he is mine,
    Now at last I can die!

I am sandaled with wind and with flame,
    I have heart-fire and singing to give,
I can tread on the grass or the stars,
    Now at last I can live!

# Riches

I have no riches but my thoughts,
    Yet these are wealth enough for me;
My thoughts of you are golden coins
    Stamped in the mint of memory;

And I must spend them all in song,
    For thoughts, as well as gold, must be
Left on the hither side of death
    To gain their immortality.

# DUSK IN WAR TIME

A half-hour more and you will lean
    To gather me close in the old sweet way—
But oh, to the woman over the sea
    Who will come at the close of day?

A half-hour more and I will hear
    The key in the latch and the strong, quick tread—
But oh, the woman over the sea
    Waiting at dusk for one who is dead!

SARA TEASDALE

# PEACE

Peace flows into me
    As the tide to the pool by the shore;
    It is mine forevermore,
It will not ebb like the sea.

I am the pool of blue
    That worships the vivid sky;
    My hopes were heaven-high,
They are all fulfilled in you.

I am the pool of gold
    When sunset burns and dies—
    You are my deepening skies;
Give me your stars to hold.

# Moods

I am the still rain falling,
    Too tired for singing mirth—
Oh, be the green fields calling,
    Oh, be for me the earth!

I am the brown bird pining
    To leave the nest and fly—
Oh, be the fresh cloud shining,
    Oh, be for me the sky!

# Houses of Dreams

You took my empty dreams
    And filled them every one
With tenderness and nobleness,
    April and the sun.

The old empty dreams
    Where my thoughts would throng
Are far too full of happiness
    To even hold a song.

Oh, the empty dreams were dim
    And the empty dreams were wide,
They were sweet and shadowy houses
    Where my thoughts could hide.

But you took my dreams away
    And you made them all come true—
My thoughts have no place now to play,
    And nothing now to do.

# Lights

When we come home at night and close the door,
    Standing together in the shadowy room,
    Safe in our own love and the gentle gloom,
Glad of familiar wall and chair and floor,

Glad to leave far below the clanging city;
    Looking far downward to the glaring street
    Gaudy with light, yet tired with many feet,
In both of us wells up a wordless pity;

Men have tried hard to put away the dark;
    A million lighted windows brilliantly
        Inlay with squares of gold the winter night,
But to us standing here there comes the stark
        Sense of the lives behind each yellow light,
    And not one wholly joyous, proud, or free.

# "I Am Not Yours"

I am not yours, not lost in you,
    Not lost, although I long to be
Lost as a candle lit at noon,
    Lost as a snowflake in the sea.

You love me, and I find you still
    A spirit beautiful and bright,
Yet I am I, who long to be
    Lost as a light is lost in light.

Oh plunge me deep in love—put out
    My senses, leave me deaf and blind,
Swept by the tempest of your love,
    A taper in a rushing wind.

# Doubt

My soul lives in my body's house,
　　And you have both the house and her—
But sometimes she is less your own
　　Than a wild, gay adventurer;
A restless and an eager wraith,
　　How can I tell what she will do—
Oh, I am sure of my body's faith,
　　But what if my soul broke faith with you?

# The Wind

A wind is blowing over my soul,
   I hear it cry the whole night through—
Is there no peace for me on earth
   Except with you?

Alas, the wind has made me wise,
   Over my naked soul it blew,—
There is no peace for me on earth
   Even with you.

# Morning

I went out on an April morning
    All alone, for my heart was high,
I was a child of the shining meadow,
    I was a sister of the sky.

There in the windy flood of morning
    Longing lifted its weight from me,
Lost as a sob in the midst of cheering,
    Swept as a sea-bird out to sea.

# OTHER MEN

When I talk with other men
    I always think of you—
Your words are keener than their words,
    And they are gentler, too.

When I look at other men,
    I wish your face were there,
With its gray eyes and dark skin
    And tossed black hair.

When I think of other men,
    Dreaming alone by day,
The thought of you like a strong wind
    Blows the dreams away.

# Embers

I said, "My youth is gone
    Like a fire beaten out by the rain,
That will never sway and sing
    Or play with the wind again."

I said, "It is no great sorrow
    That quenched my youth in me,
But only little sorrows
    Beating ceaselessly."

I thought my youth was gone,
    But you returned—
Like a flame at the call of the wind
    It leaped and burned;

Threw off its ashen cloak,
    And gowned anew
Gave itself like a bride
    Once more to you.

# Message

I heard a cry in the night,
    A thousand miles it came,
Sharp as a flash of light,
    My name, my name!

It was your voice I heard,
    You waked and loved me so—
I send you back this word,
    I know, I know!

# The Lamp

If I can bear your love like a lamp before me,
When I go down the long steep Road of Darkness,
I shall not fear the everlasting shadows,
　　Nor cry in terror.

If I can find out God, then I shall find Him,
If none can find Him, then I shall sleep soundly,
Knowing how well on earth your love sufficed me,
　　A lamp in darkness.

IV

# A November Night

There! See the line of lights,
A chain of stars down either side the street—
Why can't you lift the chain and give it to me,
A necklace for my throat? I'd twist it round
And you could play with it. You smile at me
As though I were a little dreamy child
Behind whose eyes the fairies live. . . And see,
The people on the street look up at us
All envious. We are a king and queen,
Our royal carriage is a motor bus,
We watch our subjects with a haughty joy. . .
How still you are! Have you been hard at work
And are you tired tonight? It is so long
Since I have seen you—four whole days, I think.
My heart is crowded full of foolish thoughts
Like early flowers in an April meadow,
And I must give them to you, all of them,
Before they fade. The people I have met,
The play I saw, the trivial, shifting things
That loom too big or shrink too little, shadows
That hurry, gesturing along a wall,
Haunting or gay—and yet they all grow real
And take their proper size here in my heart
When you have seen them. . . There's the Plaza now,
A lake of light! Tonight it almost seems
That all the lights are gathered in your eyes,
Drawn somehow toward you. See the open park
Lying below us with a million lamps
Scattered in wise disorder like the stars.
We look down on them as God must look down
On constellations floating under Him
Tangled in clouds. . . Come, then, and let us walk
Since we have reached the park. It is our garden,
All black and blossomless this winter night,
But we bring April with us, you and I;
We set the whole world on the trail of spring.

I think that every path we ever took
Has marked our footprints in mysterious fire,
Delicate gold that only fairies see.
When they wake up at dawn in hollow tree-trunks
And come out on the drowsy park, they look
Along the empty paths and say, "Oh, here
They went, and here, and here, and here! Come, see,
Here is their bench, take hands and let us dance
About it in a windy ring and make
A circle round it only they can cross
When they come back again!" . . . Look at the lake—
Do you remember how we watched the swans
That night in late October while they slept?
Swans must have stately dreams, I think. But now
The lake bears only thin reflected lights
That shake a little. How I long to take
One from the cold black water—new-made gold
To give you in your hand! And see, and see,
There is a star, deep in the lake, a star!
Oh, dimmer than a pearl—if you stoop down
Your hand could almost reach it up to me. . .

There was a new frail yellow moon tonight—
I wish you could have had it for a cup
With stars like dew to fill it to the brim. . .

How cold it is! Even the lights are cold;
They have put shawls of fog around them, see!
What if the air should grow so dimly white
That we would lose our way along the paths
Made new by walls of moving mist receding
The more we follow. . . What a silver night!
That was our bench the time you said to me
The long new poem—but how different now,
How eerie with the curtain of the fog
Making it strange to all the friendly trees!
There is no wind, and yet great curving scrolls
Carve themselves, ever changing, in the mist.
Walk on a little, let me stand here watching

To see you, too, grown strange to me and far. . .
I used to wonder how the park would be
If one night we could have it all alone—
No lovers with close arm-encircled waists
To whisper and break in upon our dreams.
And now we have it! Every wish comes true!
We are alone now in a fleecy world;
Even the stars have gone. We two alone!

# A Note About the Author

Sara Teasdale (1884–1933) was an American poet. Born in St. Louis, Missouri, Teasdale suffered from poor health as a child before entering school at the age of ten. In 1904, after graduating from Hosmer Hall, Teasdale joined the group of female artists known as The Potters, who published *The Potter's Wheel*, a monthly literary and visual arts magazine, from 1904 to 1907. With her first two collections—*Sonnets to Duse and Other Poems* (1907) and *Helen of Troy and Other Poems* (1911)—Teasdale earned a reputation as a gifted lyric poet from critics and readers alike. In 1916, following the publication of her bestselling *Rivers to the Sea* (1915), she moved to New York City with her husband Ernst Filsinger. There, she won the 1918 Pulitzer Prize for *Love Songs* (1917), her fourth collection. Frustrated with Filsinger's prolonged absences while traveling for work, she divorced him in 1929 and moved to another apartment in the Upper West Side. Renewing her friendship with poet Vachel Lindsay, she continued to write and publish poems until her death by suicide in 1933.

# A Note from the Publisher

Spanning many genres, from non-fiction essays to literature classics to children's books and lyric poetry, Mint Edition books showcase the master works of our time in a modern new package. The text is freshly typeset, is clean and easy to read, and features a new note about the author in each volume. Many books also include exclusive new introductory material. Every book boasts a striking new cover, which makes it as appropriate for collecting as it is for gift giving. Mint Edition books are only printed when a reader orders them, so natural resources are not wasted. We're proud that our books are never manufactured in excess and exist only in the exact quantity they need to be read and enjoyed.

# bookfinity™

## Discover more of your favorite classics with Bookfinity™.

- Track your reading with custom book lists.
- Get great book recommendations for your personalized Reader Type.
- Add reviews for your favorite books.
- AND MUCH MORE!

Visit **bookfinity.com** and take the fun Reader Type quiz to get started.

Enjoy our classic and modern companion pairings!

Classic & Modern